DRAGON'S BREATH

by Michael Gordon

THIS BOOK BELOGNS TO

....

....

George's pet dragon
is ever so neat.

Joe loves to have fun
and he loves to eat.

The two get on well
whenever they play.

But problems arise at
the end of the day.

Joe munches on snacks
until time for bed

And thinks brushing teeth
is something to dread.

"Don't like it, don't need
it, it's no fun, no way!"

So, poor George is stuck
at the end of the day.

The smell in the room
is incredibly strong

George tenderly says, "Joe,
I don't know what's wrong

But your breath has become
seriously rotten.

Did you eat bad cheese and
somehow forgotten?

He said it in jest, but that's what he thinks.

"You hurt my feelings; your joke is what stinks!"

"Sorry," George says, "It's just that I care.

When Mom tucks us in I don't want her scared."

Joe doesn't believe that his teeth should be clean,

Till a day later, when they start turning green.

Whenever the boys play, George laughs and smiles.

But poor Joe keeps his mouth closed all the while.

Joe feels bad about
the horrible sight.

So, George decides to try
something new that night.

He wants to show Joe
that brushing is fun.

To succeed, Joe has to
win the competition.

Joe loves to compete
so he's sure to try.

George feels a bit bad
that he has to be sly,

But he knows Joe's unhappy;
the smell is so bad.

Joe's taken the "House
Smelliest" title from Dad.

That night, George turns bedtime into a race.

The first to clean his teeth and wash his face

Will choose bedtime stories for the whole week.

Joe is excited but too embarrassed to speak.

The race starts and George
makes sure not to win.

Joe finishes and gives a
huge crocodile grin.

"That was fun!" he says.
"My teeth are so clean!"

"Your teeth sparkle," says
George, "and have a white sheen."

"I've missed your smiles,
Joe, and your chatter too.

Cleaning teeth can be fun,
a great thing to do."

Good hygiene is important,
Joe finally sees.

"I'm the best teeth cleaner!"
he cheers, and George agrees.

About author

Michael Gordon is the talented author of several highly rated children's books including the popular Sleep Tight, Little Monster, and the Animal Bedtime.

He collaborates with the renowned Kids Book Book that creates picture books for all of ages to enjoy. Michael's goal is to create books that are engaging, funny, and inspirational for children of all ages and their parents.

Contact

For all other questions about books or author, please e-mail michaelgordonclub@gmail.com.

Award-winning books

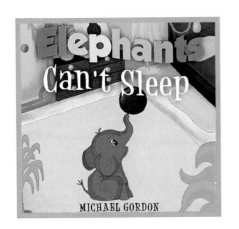

Elephants Can not Sleep

The

Little Elephant likes to break the rules. He never cleans his room. He never listens to mama's bedtime stories and goes to bed really late. But what if he tried to follow the routine so that the bedtime would become an amazing experience?

Little Girl's Daddy

the Who Needs a super hero the when you have your dad? Written in beautiful rhyme this is an excellent story that honors all fathers in the world.

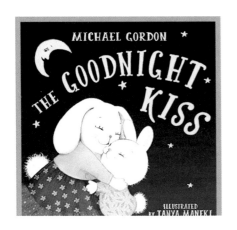

The Goodnight Kiss

Welcome to a cozy, sweet little bunny family. Mom is putting her little son Ben to bed, but she's not quite successful. Little boy still wants to play games and stay up late. Ben also likes to keep his mommy in his room at bedtime. Mrs. Bunny tries milk, warm blankets, books , and finally a kiss ... what will work?

My Big Brother

The

Each of our lives will always be a special part of the other. There's Nothing Quite Like A Sibling Bond Written in beautiful rhyme this is an excellent story that values patience, acceptance and bond between a brother and his sister.

Made in the USA
Las Vegas, NV
15 November 2021